## JUMP-STARTING A CAREER IN

# MENTAL HEALTH AND THERAPY

## CORONA BREZINA

Rosen
**YA**™

New York

Published in 2019 by The Rosen Publishing Group, Inc.
29 East 21st Street, New York, NY 10010

Copyright © 2019 by The Rosen Publishing Group, Inc.

First Edition

**Library of Congress Cataloging-in-Publication Data**

Names: Brezina, Corona, author.
Title: Jump-starting a career in mental health and therapy / Corona Brezina.
Description: First edition. | New York : Rosen YA, 2019. | Series: Health care careers in 2 years | Audience: Grades 7–12. | Includes bibliographical references and index.
Identifiers: LCCN 2018007105| ISBN 9781508184997 (library bound) | ISBN 9781508184980 (paperback)
Subjects: LCSH: Mental health personnel—Vocational guidance—Juvenile literature. | Youth—Tobacco use—Juvenile literature.
Classification: LCC RC440.8 .B74 2019 | DDC 616.890092—dc23
LC record available at https://lccn.loc.gov/2018007105

*Manufactured in the United States of America*

# CONTENTS

# INTRODUCTION

**M**orning on the pediatric ward of a psychiatric hospital begins early with a hot breakfast for patients. The patients on the pediatric ward are children ranging from five to seventeen years old. They have been admitted because of severe mental health issues. They may be suffering from psychosis and lose touch with reality. They may represent a threat to themselves or others. Some may have overdosed on drugs before being admitted.

The psychiatric technicians charged with providing direct care for the patients have already begun to prepare for the day's work. They've reviewed the patient records from the previous shift. They assist patients with one of their first activities in the morning: setting personal treatment goals for the day. After breakfast, the psychiatric technicians might take the patients to the gym for an exercise period. Other activities on the tightly structured schedule may include academic classes, recreational therapy, journaling sessions, time in the art room, and group therapy—psychiatric technicians sometimes lead the sessions. Unplanned activities could involve defusing a patient's tantrum or preventing a patient from trying to run away.

Throughout the day, psychiatric technicians frequently make note of patients' moods, monitor what the patients eat and whether they sleep well, take the patients to their activities for the day, and prepare the patients for appointments

Good communication skills are essential for professionals who work in the field of mental health. Psychiatric technicians and aides, for example, spend much of their time interacting with patients.

with the psychiatrist. Psychiatric technicians also admit patients, which involves taking a medical history and listening to the concerns of both parents and children. They inventory the patients' possessions, remove any contraband, and complete the necessary paperwork—a psychiatric technician's work involves maintaining and updating highly precise and detailed medical records.

As the day winds down, the patients have visiting hours with parents and other family members. They review their progress on their goals for the day and get ready for bed.

The therapeutic environment and medical treatment is effective in treating young patients in crisis. Within a matter of days, most patients will have stabilized enough to be sent home with an outpatient care plan.

Psychiatric technicians represent an example of a mental health care career that is essential for patient care and personally fulfilling yet requires two or fewer years of education and training. They may hold a postsecondary certificate or associate's degree in psychiatric or mental health technology.

Mental health care, like many fields within health care, is experiencing expansion and job growth. For new entrants to the workforce, health care can offer secure jobs that don't necessarily require expensive four-year degrees. Entry-level workers with an associate's degree or less can enter the field of mental health care as, for example, a psychiatric technician or substance abuse counselor. Mental health care is a challenging and rewarding field in which compassionate professionals provide patients with treatment that can help them recover from mental health crises and manage long-term mental illness.

# Chapter 1

# WORKING IN THE FIELD OF MENTAL HEALTH

**M**ental health professionals treat medical problems related to patients' emotional, psychological, and social health. Mental health is a wide-ranging field, and cases of mental illness are much more common than most people realize. According to the National Alliance on Mental Illness, about one out of five adults in the United States struggles with mental illness in any given year. These disorders range from manageable mental health concerns, such as an anxiety disorder, to serious long-term conditions, such as the mental illness schizophrenia.

Mental illness is treated by a variety of professionals who specialize in different roles in the mental health care system. Psychiatrists and psychologists diagnose and treat serious mental illness. Psychiatrists are medical doctors who can prescribe medication, while psychologists generally are not allowed to write prescriptions. Both psychiatrists and psychologists treat patients with psychotherapy, in which they talk with patients to help them resolve their problems.

Counselors and therapists also treat mental health problems. The specific descriptions and requirements of job positions in counseling vary from one state to another. Counselors often focus on specific concerns, such as substance abuse or family treatment. Psychologists are sometimes categorized as counselors, but there are educational programs that specifically train licensed professional counselors as well.

Likewise, "therapist" is a broad term that can describe a variety of mental health professionals—from psychologists to marriage counselors to life coaches—who provide people with guidance for the problems in their lives.

These specialists are almost always highly trained and educated, possessing a bachelor's degree and often a master's, doctorate, or medical degree. However, they are supported by a wide range of personnel who help treat patients and coordinate their care.

## Overview of the Field

Mental health conditions can be treated in many types of settings and involve a variety of different mental health professionals. When someone begins to realize that he or she may be suffering from a mental health issue, that person may first turn to self-help resources— such as books or websites—to learn more about what's wrong. He or she might also seek out a support group or make an appointment with a mental health professional. Treatment providers include facilities such as private practices, community mental health centers, and substance abuse treatment centers. Unless a person is in crisis, any treatment will probably be outpatient—he or she will visit a therapist or other professional for treatment sessions rather than being hospitalized.

People suffering from severe mental illness may benefit from inpatient or residential treatment, in which they are admitted to a hospital or other facility for close monitoring and intensive treatment. Residential treatment provides a structured environment in which patients can concentrate on addressing their mental health. The goal of inpatient treatment is to stabilize patients and put them onto a path of recovery so that they can manage their mental illness and return to their daily lives. Some substance abuse treatment programs also involve a period of inpatient treatment.

Larger facilities treating patients with severe mental health issues employ a greater number and variety of mental health personnel than smaller practices or clinics

Mental health facilities provide patients with a secure and supportive environment in which counselors and other mental health workers can administer appropriate care and treatment.

providing outpatient services. Mental health professionals are also needed at facilities that treat patients with serious mental and physical health conditions that prevent them from living independently—for example, people with severe developmental or intellectual disabilities or older adults suffering from diseases such as dementia. Such patients often require both medical and mental health care.

Mental health care can be a challenging as well as a rewarding field of work. One of the most important personal traits for any mental health care professional is a sense of compassion for patients suffering from mental illness. There are many common misconceptions about mental illness, and people suffering from mental health issues often feel stigmatized by the people around them. Mental health professionals must be able to assure patients that mental illness is not a result of weakness or personal failing. Patients who succeed in managing their mental illness can lead fulfilling and productive lives. Their recovery is often made possible by mental health professionals who understand their needs and are able to provide effective treatment.

## Psychiatric Technician

Psychiatric technicians are the mental health care workers who spend the most time interacting with patients in a mental health care setting. Psychiatric technicians work under the supervision of medical personnel such as psychiatrists, other medical doctors, psychologists, and nursing staff. They are generally considered a specialized type of nursing aide. Alternate job titles include mental health assistant and psychiatric nursing assistant.

Psychiatric technicians assist mental health patients who are not capable of caring for themselves. These may include children, adults, or geriatric adults who have severe mental illness, developmental disabilities, or drug or alcohol addiction. Psychiatric technicians are involved in patients' treatment plans and attend to their daily well-being. They also perform basic medical duties, such as administering medication or checking a patient's temperature or blood pressure.

Psychiatric technicians are charged with direct care of mental health care patients. They assist with tasks related to daily life and hygiene, such as feeding and bathing. They lead and participate in therapeutic and recreational activities. They arrange transportation and accompany patients to appointments and outings such as visits to movie theaters or museums. Psychiatric technicians play card games with patients, watch TV with them, teach life skills, and interact socially with them. Psychiatric technicians are expected to serve as role models in encouraging positive social behavior. In some settings, they establish a rapport with patients to encourage rehabilitation—restoring them to a healthy mental state.

Because psychiatric technicians have extended contact with patients on a daily basis, their observations are important in evaluating a patient's recovery and the effectiveness of treatment plans. Psychiatric technicians help keep medical records, and they report any significant changes, such as reactions to medications or troubling behavior that might require an intervention. Higher-level psychiatric technicians may admit and discharge patients, and they may serve as liaisons with patients' families and provide relevant education concerning the patient's

Detailed, accurate medical records are essential for tracking a patient's long-term progress. Psychiatric technicians record notes regarding any relevant health information or observations.

condition. Depending on the program, they may continue to monitor a patient's ongoing progress after the patient is released from inpatient treatment.

Psychiatric technicians often deal with patients with severe mental illnesses who may represent a danger to themselves or others. They may be required to calm a disturbed patient, deal with emergencies, or even restrain a patient physically. The job can sometimes be dangerous for the psychiatric technician—the incidence rate of violence in the workplace is thirty-eight times higher for psychiatric technicians than the national rate, according to the Bureau of Labor Statistics (BLS). Psychiatric technicians also experience an occupational injury and illness rate that is four times higher than the national rate.

Psychiatric technicians must possess compassion, patience, and keen observational skills for monitoring patients' behavior. Good communication skills are also essential. Psychiatric technicians must relate well to patients in addition to being able to discuss relevant medical issues with other mental health care personnel and explain the patient's status to family members. In addition, psychiatric technicians often spend a great deal of their time on their feet throughout the workday. The job may also require physical strength if they have to help lift patients.

Psychiatric technicians held about 66,100 jobs in 2016, according to a BLS report on January 30, 2018. The largest employers were psychiatric and substance abuse hospitals, including state, local, and private facilities, which employed about 42 percent of psychiatric technicians.

About 16 percent were employed by private general medical and surgical hospitals, and about 10 percent by state governments (excluding education and hospitals). The remaining 13 percent worked at mental health and substance abuse facilities, including both inpatient and outpatient treatment. (These could be smaller facilities than hospitals and might target specific needs and offer inpatient or outpatient care.) Psychiatric technicians may work either full time or part time. Because some facilities must be staffed twenty-four hours a day, the job may involve working overnight and weekend shifts.

# A DAY IN THE LIFE: MEET TONI

Toni works as a licensed psychiatric technician in a hospital in Sacramento, California.
She helps care for patients with bipolar,
personality, and schizophrenic disorders.
Toni completed an eighteen-month training
program to qualify for her license. Two of
Toni's answers to questions about her job,
quoted from the Health Jobs Start Here
website (http://www.healthjobsstarthere
.com/dayinthelife/toni), are as follows:

*What's your favorite part of the job?*
It's amazing to see the improvement in my
patients' health. They usually come in really
mentally disorganized and I watch their
condition stabilize day after day all because
of the care I give them. And the bond I form
with them is so meaningful to me. Some of
my patients share stories about their lives—
sometimes funny, sometimes sad. It helps
me understand where they're coming from
and provide better care.

*What's most challenging?*
Being a psych tech is definitely not easy.
Two patients could be diagnosed with iden-
tical conditions but require different

**treatments. I have to try different combinations of medicines andrelationship-building styles until I see positive results. The feeling I get when I eventually get it right is priceless.**

According to the 2018 BLS report, the median annual wage for psychiatric technicians was $30,970. Employment was projected to grow about 6 percent from 2016 to 2026, which is about average among all occupations. As the number of older Americans requiring mental health care increases, demand for the services of psychiatric technicians is expected to grow.

## Psychiatric Aide

Psychiatric aide is a common title for an entry-level psychiatric technician. Psychiatric aides perform many of the same duties as psychiatric technicians, but they are generally assigned lower-level responsibilities. Rather than taking part in therapeutic aspects of patients' routines, they are more likely to help patients with everyday functioning and oversee recreational and educational activities. They may attend to housekeeping duties, such as changing bed linens and cleaning patients' rooms. Often, psychiatric aides encourage patients to take responsibility for performing basic hygiene and cleaning tasks themselves to promote independence.

As is the case for psychiatric technicians, the job can sometimes be dangerous—according to a BLS March 2015 labor review article, the incidence rate of violence in the workplace is sixty-nine times higher for psychiatric

Psychiatric aides may be required to help patients with meals, personal hygiene, and other aspects of daily life that they can't manage on their own.

aides than the national rate. Psychiatric aides also experienced an occupational injury and illness rate that was seven times higher than the national rate.

Psychiatric aides held about 73,600 jobs in 2016, according to the January 2018 BLS report. The largest employers were psychiatric and substance abuse hospitals, including state, local, and private facilities, which employed about 40 percent of psychiatric aides.

About 25 percent are employed by state governments (excluding education and hospitals). Other major employers include residential facilities for those with intellectual and developmental disabilities, residential mental health and substance abuse facilities (usually defined as centers for short- or long-term, generally voluntary, treatment in which patients live), and private general medical and surgical hospitals.

According to the January 2018 BLS report, the median annual wage for psychiatric aides in 2016 was $26,720. Employment was projected to grow about 6 percent from 2016 to 2026, which is about average among all occupations.

## Substance Abuse Counselor

Substance abuse counselors are professionals who provide treatment to people who are addicted to drugs or alcohol. Alternate job titles include addiction counselor or alcohol and drug abuse counselor. Most mental health counselors are required to have bachelor's or advanced degrees, but some states license substance abuse counselors who complete an associate's degree. Be sure to check the relevant requirements in your state if you're considering a career as a substance abuse counselor.

Substance abuse counselors help patients overcome their dependence on drugs and alcohol. Addiction is considered a disease—addicts feel compelled to continue using drugs or alcohol regardless of the damaging consequences the behavior has on their lives and health. Many addicts are unable to stop using drugs or alcohol on their own and require treatment by substance abuse counselors in order to recover from addiction.

An addict's first step toward recovery is admitting that he or she has a problem with drug or alcohol abuse. In some cases, a patient may be compelled to enter treatment by concerned relatives or the law, and he or she may not be ready to accept that the problem is out of control. A substance abuse counselor's role begins with an assessment of the patient's mental and physical health, substance use, and readiness for treatment.

Patients have many different treatment options, and a number of different factors affect what type of treatment program they enter. People with severe drug addictions may have to undergo detoxification to treat physical dependency. Addicts who have been unsuccessful in previous attempts to break their addiction may choose to enter an inpatient treatment program, with a structured regimen focusing on rehabilitation, rather than outpatient services. Cost or availability may also be a factor for some people, in which case substance abuse counselors will need to take such limitations into consideration.

The substance abuse counselor's role is to provide motivation and support throughout the process. A substance abuse counselor generally works as part of a team that includes doctors, psychiatrists, psychologists, nursing staff, and social workers. The team will put together a treatment plan for the patient and begin the process of rehabilitation. Possible recommendations include inpatient or outpatient treatment, medication, twelve-step plans, peer support, case management, and follow-up services. Therapy—both individual and group—is invaluable for the recovery process. The substance abuse counselor will help the patient develop skills and behaviors that will help ensure a successful recovery. The patient will learn to identify and avoid behaviors and situations that may lead to relapse, and he or she may need to repair relationships and employment situations that were damaged by addiction. A substance abuse counselor also meets with family members, refers patients to recovery support services such as support groups or employment services, monitors patients' progress, and keeps records related to their case. Substance abuse counselors also do outreach work to educate the public about the dangers of addiction.

A substance abuse counselor may specialize in a particular type of treatment. Some counselors may deal with a specific type of patient, such as teenagers, women, or veterans. Others may specialize in treating a

During a substance abuse group therapy session, patients benefit from the guidance of a trained counselor as well as the support of peers who share their personal experiences.

specific type of addiction, such as alcoholism or dependency on opioids, cocaine, or methamphetamine.

A substance abuse counselor must be compassionate, nonjudgmental, and patient. Good communication skills are essential, and listening and responding to a patient's concerns is particularly important.

Substance abuse counselors work in a variety of settings, including residential treatment centers, outpatient treatment centers, hospitals, private practice, mental health centers, halfway houses, detoxification centers, and community service organizations. Employers include both private facilities and government agencies. Substance abuse counselors generally work full time, and they may experience heavy caseloads.

According to the 2018 BLS report, the median annual wage for substance abuse counselors was $41,070. Employment was projected to grow about 23 percent from 2016 to 2026—significantly above average among all occupations. Growing numbers of people are seeking help for addictions, and the justice system is increasingly sentencing drug offenders to treatment programs as an alternative to sending them to jail.

# Chapter 2

# RELATED HEALTH CARE OPPORTUNITIES

**T**he therapists and counselors who treat mental illness are supported by health care professionals who specialize in various other general medical specialties that are nonetheless essential for the care of mental health patients. Mental hospitals, residential facilities, substance abuse programs, and other settings that provide mental health care also require personnel to manage the office, perform patient care, oversee health information such as medical records, and dispense medications.

For these professionals, training or experience working with mental health patients can serve as a valuable career asset. Working in a mental health care setting can be challenging as well as highly rewarding. Potential employers are likely to take note of job candidates who have demonstrated that they possess the knowledge and skill set necessary to succeed in helping mental health patients work toward recovery. Conversely, working in a mental health care workplace can open new windows of opportunity for employees, too. General medical personnel might find that they have an aptitude and an interest in a mental health career, and they may decide to pursue formal training in a mental health care specialization.

## Medical Secretary or Administrative Assistant

Medical secretaries, also called medical administrative assistants, attend to the clerical tasks in a doctor's office, hospital, or other medical facility. Their organizational role is crucial in keeping an office running smoothly. Medical secretaries interact with patients in the office, answer the phone, make appointments, handle mail, and

Medical receptionists welcome patients and address their questions, whether in person, by telephone, or over email. Other tasks include scheduling appointments and managing records.

update documents and databases. In addition to these standard administrative skills, medical secretaries need to be familiar with medical terminology and codes as well as the details of hospital or laboratory procedures for their work. They may be required to manage insurance information, manage medical charts and records, and bill patients.

Training for secretarial and administrative work is available at technical schools and community colleges, although some high-school graduates learn the necessary skills through on-the-job training. Additional course work in medical terminology is recommended for medical secretaries.

## Medical Assistant

Medical assistants perform a variety of administrative and clinical duties in health care settings. Medical assistants work under the supervision of doctors and nurses. Medical assistants may answer phones and greet patients as well as take medical histories and prepare patients for an examination. However, medical assistants are not the same as physician assistants, who are trained to diagnose and treat patients.

Many medical assistants work in doctor's offices or clinics that are not large enough to require separate personnel for various office and clinical duties. A medical assistant may assist the doctor during procedures, order and stock medical supplies, administer medications to patients, prepare blood samples for testing, keep waiting areas and examination rooms clean, sterilize instruments, and explain treatments to patients. Administrative

Medical assistants perform clinical duties and also attend to administrative tasks, such as taking inventory of medical supplies at a mental health clinic.

responsibilities may include bookkeeping, record keeping, scheduling appointments, arranging for prescriptions to be filled, and dealing with insurance companies. Specific tasks will vary depending on the size and specialization of the practice. In addition, state law may specify what types of clinical duties can be performed by medical assistants. Some specialized medical assistants are trained to work in a particular area of medicine.

Most medical assistants complete a one- or two-year program at a community college or other institution and

# SOCIAL SERVICES AIDE

Mental health care is relevant to the field of social work, which is concerned with helping people overcome challenges in their lives. Social workers often help people deal with mental health conditions, but they also address other issues, such as poverty, physical health problems, unemployment, family troubles, abuse, or access to education. In addition, rather than dealing solely with an individual client, social workers may also reach out to communities, organizations, and government service providers to resolve social problems.

Social workers generally have at least a bachelor's degree. However, social services aides with qualifications such as a relevant associate's degree or on-the-job training assist social workers. Alternate job titles include casework aide, family service assistant, addictions counselor assistant, and human service worker. There are many subfields of social work, such as child and family social work, health care social work, and mental health and substance abuse social work. Social services aides help identify appropriate assistance for clients, assist in drawing up treatment plans, work to

(continued on the next page)

*(continued from the previous page)*

**coordinate services, gather data for statistical purposes, and act as a liaison with community groups. A social services aide often provides basic help with tasks that the client can't manage, such as filling in forms or arranging transportation. Social services aides may work in offices, clinics, hospitals, residential care facilities, and shelters, and they may travel to visit clients. In 2016, the median pay for a social services aides was $31,810, according to a January 2018 BLS report, although pay will vary greatly, depending on geographical area and type of employment. Job outlook was bright, with growth expected to increase faster than average—16 percent from 2016 to 2026.**

earn a certificate or an associate's degree in the field. Some medical assistants with only a high school degree learn through on-the-job training.

## Licensed Practical Nurse (LPN)

Licensed practical nurses provide basic nursing care to patients in nursing and residential care facilities, hospitals, doctor's offices, and other health care settings. They may also provide home health care services. In some states, they are called licensed vocational nurses (LVNs).

Licensed practical nurses monitor patients, check vital signs such as pulse and temperature, change bandages,

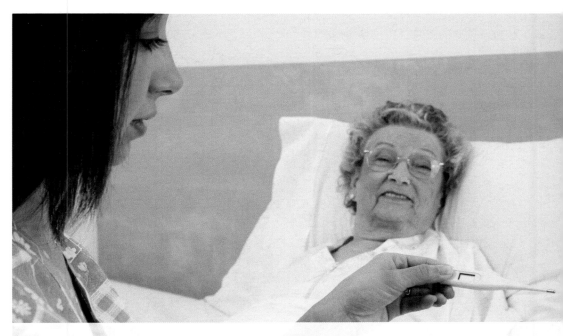

Licensed practical nurses are employed in a wide variety of health care settings. LPNs who provide home health care services can help patients maintain independence and self-sufficiency.

and maintain records. They also help feed, bathe, and dress patients. A licensed practical nurse's duties depend on state laws—for example, not all states allow them to administer medications, and laws in some states require a greater extent of direct supervision by registered nurses (RNs). Depending on the setting, some licensed practical nurses may specialize in a certain area of medicine.

Training programs for licensed practical nurses are offered at technical schools, community colleges, hospitals, and universities, and most take only a year to complete. Some high schools even offer practical nursing programs.

## Registered Nurse (RN)

Registered nurses make up the largest category of health care personnel in the medical system. Over half of all registered nurses work in hospitals. Other employers include doctor's offices, clinics, residential facilities, and schools.

Registered nurses monitor patients and track their progress toward recovery. They assess patients' conditions, set up plans for care based on a doctor's prescribed treatment plans, and work as part of a team to provide direct care. Registered nurses administer medications, operate medical equipment, assist with medical tests, and update medical records. They also educate patients about their health conditions, answer questions, provide emotional support to patients and their families, and explain how to manage their health following discharge.

Registered nurses perform a wide range of duties, depending on specialization and setting. There are many areas of nursing—registered nurses may work with a particular type of patient, such as geriatric (elderly) patients, or specialize in a particular setting, such as the operating room or a rehabilitation facility. Two specializations relevant to mental health are psychiatric nurses and addiction nurses, also called substance abuse nurses. In addition to providing direct care, nurses work in areas such as administration, consulting, and research.

Educational options for registered nurses include a two-year program leading to an associate's degree, a two- or three-year hospital diploma program, or a bachelor's degree in nursing from a college or university. Students interested in pursuing a nursing career in the mental health field should take relevant courses related to mental health as well as general medicine. Taking psychiatric clinical courses is also beneficial.

## Nursing Assistant

Nursing assistants, also called nursing aides or hospital attendants, provide basic care to patients, often under the supervision of a registered nurse or licensed practical nurse. Most nursing assistants work in residential facilities such as nursing care facilities, retirement communities, and assisted living facilities. Nursing assistants also work in hospitals.

Some nursing assistants provide basic care to geriatric patients, who may suffer from mental health issues such as depression or Alzheimer's disease in addition to physical health conditions.

Nursing assistants attend to the everyday needs of patients. They assist in feeding, dressing, and bathing patients. They take vital signs such as temperature and blood pressure, reposition patients in bed, help patients move from a bed to a wheelchair, and transport patients. In facilities such as nursing homes, nursing assistants often serve as the primary caregiver to residents. They may establish personal relationships with patients, and they are charged with informing doctors or nurses about any changes in a patient's condition.

Nursing assistants must hold a high school diploma and complete a training program. Training programs are offered at community colleges, technical schools, hospitals, and nursing homes, as well as some high schools. A nursing assistant may complete course work simultaneously with on-the-job training after being hired.

## Orderly

Orderlies, sometimes called ward assistants, perform largely nonmedical duties related to patient care. Most orderlies work in hospitals under the supervision of doctors and nurses.

Orderlies transport or help patients move around the hospital. They stock supplies, change bed linens, and keep facilities and equipment clean. An orderly's duties can overlap with those of a nursing assistant—orderlies may help patients with basic tasks and hygiene.

Orderlies must hold a high school diploma. Generally, they receive on-the-job training.

## Pharmacy Technician

Pharmacy technicians, also called pharmacy assistants or pharmacy technologists, work under pharmacists, who dispense medication and advise patients on appropriate use. Most pharmacy technicians work in pharmacies or drugstores, but hospitals also employ pharmacy technicians.

Pharmacy technicians measure, mix, package, and label amounts of medication. They take inventory of the pharmacy's stock and inform the pharmacist when any supplies are running low. Pharmacy technicians may deal with customers and update medical and insurance records, but they do not instruct patients on medications or health issues. In hospitals and other health care facilities, pharmacy technicians may deliver prescriptions to different units or departments.

A job as a pharmacy technician requires a high degree of precision and attention to detail, even when the technician may feel under pressure to work quickly.

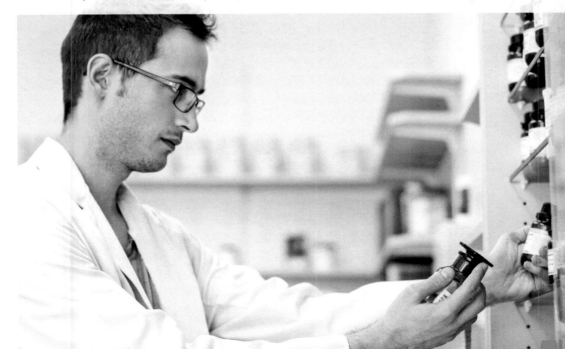

Pharmacy technicians must hold a high school diploma. Some learn on the job by starting out as pharmacy aides, but most complete a training program at a community college or technical school. Programs typically take a year or less to complete, although some pharmacy technicians study for two years and earn an associate's degree. Students learn about different medications and their characteristics, as well as pharmaceutical mathematics, law, and record keeping. Some programs also involve an internship or other hands-on work experience in a pharmacy.

## Health Information Technician

Health information technicians, also called medical records technicians or medical records associates, organize and manage health information. Health information technicians confer with doctors and nurses to ensure that records are accurate, but they typically have minimal contact with patients. Most health information technicians work in hospitals or doctor's offices.

Health information technicians ensure that patient records are accurate and complete, including diagnosis and procedure codes. Health information is used for many purposes beyond individual patient care. The codes are used for insurance reimbursement and for data analysis. Tracking patient outcomes can help hospitals improve care, for example, or cut costs. Health information is also reported to government agencies for public health purposes and to hold medical facilities accountable. Health information technicians should understand the Health Insurance Portability and Accountability Act (HIPAA) of

1996 that allows professionals to share protected health information for treatment purposes. Health information technicians should be able to interpret compliance rules that protect the privacy of people's health information.

Health information practices are constantly being updated and transformed because of new regulations and advances in technology. Anyone interested in pursuing a career as a health information technician should be prepared to stay current with the latest trends.

Most health information technicians hold a certificate or an associate's degree in health information technology from a community or junior college. Students take classes on medical subjects as well as health data, health care statistics, and computers.

## Medical Transcriptionist

Medical transcriptionists, also known as health care documentation specialists, listen to dictation (a voice recording) and type the information into a document—a transcript. Medical transcriptionists typically work in the medical records departments of hospitals, companies that provide transcription services, or doctors' offices.

Medical transcriptionists must be able to provide accurate transcripts that use medical terminology correctly. They must also double-check patient information, such as addresses and spellings of names, and submit documents to doctors and other personnel for approval. A medical transcriptionist may utilize speech recognition technology as well—instead of listening to and transcribing the entire recording, he or she may review and edit a draft created by computer software.

Some medical transcriptionists specialize in providing services to mental health professionals. They must be familiar with terminology related to mental health conditions and treatments.

Most medical transcriptionists complete a training program in medical transcription and earn a certificate or associate's degree. Required course work includes anatomy, medical terminology, legal issues, and English.

## Job Outlook and Pay in Health Care

Health care makes up the fastest-growing set of occupations in the American economy. The general population of the country is growing older, and demand for health care services is expected to rise. People who are elderly generally require more health care, and mental health issues related to aging will also increase.

The BLS projected in its January 2018 report that about 2.4 million new health care jobs would be added to the economy from 2016 to 2026. Employment of medical assistants, medical secretaries, and registered nurses is expected to grow much faster than average for all occupations. Employment of licensed practical and licensed vocational nurses, pharmacy technicians, health information technicians, and nursing assistants is projected to grow faster than the average.

In 2016, the median pay for health care support jobs was $27,910, according to the 2018 BLS report. Among health care support jobs relevant to mental health care, median pay ranged from $26,590 for nursing assistants, to $33,730 for medical secretaries, to $44,090 for licensed practical and licensed vocational nurses. The median pay for registered nurses was $68,450, but registered nurses with an associate's degree will typically earn less than those with a bachelor's degree or higher.

# Chapter 3

# GETTING A HEALTH CARE EDUCATION

**S**ome health care jobs require only a high school diploma, but additional education and training can expand job prospects and long-term career outlook. You should take your mental health care education and training very seriously. Medical personnel and counselors are responsible for the recovery and well-being of the patients under their care. It is an important job, and good-quality educational and training programs ensure that graduates are fully prepared to carry out their duties. Health care jobs generally require medical skills, such as taking vital signs and updating patient charts, as well as "soft skills," such as good communication and the ability to put a patient at ease. Education and training typically involve both classroom learning and practical experience dealing with patients.

## *High School Preparation*

A good work ethic is essential for a successful health care career. Laying a foundation for optimal job performance can start with sound academic choices and hard work in high school.

Aspiring mental health care workers should take a wide range of high school science and math classes. Knowledge of biology is fundamental in the field of health care, and you should sign up for courses in anatomy, psychology, sociology, and health if your school offers them. Good communication skills are essential for a mental health care worker, so you should take classes in English and computers. The government—on federal, state, and local levels—employs a significant number of mental health care workers, and personnel working for private mental health facilities often deal with government

Take a variety of science classes in high school—health care careers require that you have a sound understanding of how the human body works.

agencies. Taking classes in government and economics can provide useful background knowledge.

Vocational-technical (vo-tech) institutions can also offer great opportunities for students to obtain practical skills during high school. Many vo-tech programs offer a general course in health care, while others train students for a specific occupation. A student studying to become a nursing assistant, for example, may receive a diploma, a license, and certification upon completing the program. Graduates of vo-tech programs may be able to find jobs in their field straight out of high school or else use their vo-tech course work as a foundation for continuing their mental health care education. Some vo-tech institutions may partner with colleges, universities, or hospitals, too. A high school student may be able to earn college credit toward a degree or explore clinical opportunities in a hospital setting along with classroom study.

Extracurricular and volunteer activities can boost your prospects for a career in mental health, too. Does your school offer a science fair, a debate team, or student government? Consider doing volunteer work, especially in settings that offer relevant experience to prospective health care workers, such as community service organizations or hospitals. Hospital staff members often offer encouragement and opportunities for practical involvement to young volunteers who are interested in pursuing health care careers.

An after-school or summer job can also provide a chance to acquire new skills as well as earn money. This kind of work experience looks good on job applications and résumés because it demonstrates that a candidate can handle responsibility and balance school, work, and personal life. Consider applying for jobs such as entry-level or trainee positions as a psychiatric aide, nursing aide, or student tutor in a school program for children with developmental delays.

## Mental Health Care Education and Training

Once you've identified your dream job in mental health care, the next step is to map out possible educational paths. Some basic health care jobs require only a high school degree followed by on-the-job training, while

During on-the-job training, psychiatric technicians learn workplace routines, duties, and safety procedures under the supervision of an experienced staff member.

others require at least an associate's degree. For some jobs, there are multiple options for training programs. In pursuing a career as a medical assistant, for example, you might choose to earn either a certificate or diploma through a one-year program or an associate's degree through a two-year program. The certificate or diploma would enable you to get a job more quickly. The associate's degree might qualify you for a greater range of better-paying jobs, but it would take longer to complete. In making your educational decisions, you need to weigh both your short-term and long-term priorities. Double-check your state's requirements for certification and licensing as well.

The next step is to apply for a program. You need to research potential institutions to ensure that they're reputable. In many health care fields, a person must graduate from an accredited school to qualify to take the examination for a license. Make sure that your program is state approved. Apply well in advance, too, since slots in some high-demand programs may be filled quickly, and look into whether you might qualify for financial aid such as scholarships, grants, and loans.

Many students pursuing health care careers choose to enroll in a regional community college. Community colleges can provide a high-quality, affordable education in practical career areas. Class schedules are often more flexible for students at community colleges as compared to universities. They are more likely to offer night classes, for example, allowing students to work while attending school part time.

Once you are enrolled, make a solid commitment to your studies. Despite providing a solid education,

# DRAFTING A RÉSUMÉ AND CRAFTING A COVER LETTER

A job application generally includes a résumé and cover letter. You should start building your résumé while you're still in school and update it regularly.

A résumé is a document that summarizes your professional qualifications. All résumés include contact information and sections on education and work experience. You can also include sections on activities, awards, credentials, interests, skills, or volunteer service that might be pertinent to the job. Some résumés include an objective at the beginning and references at the end. There are several different formats for résumés, and you should research the standard format for the field of health care. If possible, ask a career counselor to review your résumé. He or she can proofread it for errors, help you with formatting, and give tips on improving the content.

When applying for a job, you should research the employer and tailor your résumé to highlight skills and achievements applicable to the position. If you're applying for a psychiatric technician job at a residential facility, for example, describe skills you learned during an internship at a hospital. Include keywords relevant to the job description that

*(continued on the next page)*

*(continued from the previous page)*

**are likely to grab the employer's attention. Pay attention to any specific submission requirements in the job description.**

**The cover letter is another important element of a job application. Your cover letter gives you a chance to introduce yourself and make the case that you're a great candidate for the specific job. Emphasize why your qualifications match the requirements for the job. An effective cover letter can grab your prospective employer's attention and make you stand out from the rest of the applicants. Include a cover letter with every job application unless the description specifically requests that you do not send one.**

community colleges have a lower graduation rate than four-year schools. You can succeed by developing good habits from the start. Establish a relationship with your academic adviser, and consult him or her about choosing classes and balancing your various responsibilities. See if you can sign up for a "student success class" that teaches skills such as time management and study skills. Make sure that you attend every class and turn in every assignment on time. Participate during class, and take advantage of your professors' office hours to ask for help or career advice.

## *Enhancing Your Qualifications*

The prospect of searching for a first job after completing a training program can be daunting. Take advantage of any opportunities for hands-on job experience that come your way. Many educational programs require an internship or a stint of supervised work as a trainee, which may be described as field experience or externship. In some cases, this training period can lead to a job offer.

Seek out a mentor who can provide guidance as you complete your education and embark on your career. A mentor is an experienced professional in the field who can listen to your concerns and share expertise. A

To gain accreditation, a substance abuse counselor generally must complete a minimum amount of supervised work experience spent treating patients.

relationship with a mentor is friendly but generally more formal and respectful than your friendships with peers. Your mentor may be an adviser at your school or a supervisor at a work-study program. Professional organizations may also have mentoring programs that connect entry-level workers to experienced professionals in the field.

Many fields of health care require that a candidate be licensed or certified to work in the profession. The licensing requirements set by a state board will typically involve a certain level of specialized education, a minimum amount of job experience, and passing an exam administered by a national board or association that sets standards for the field. Some training programs incorporate the certification exam into the course schedule.

Not all fields within health care require certification or licensing, but attaining such credentials can be beneficial even when it is not absolutely necessary. Certification provides proof of a certain level of professional competence. Some professions offer an entry-level certification as well as certifications for higher levels or specialized skills. Nursing assistants, for example, are required to pass an exam qualifying them as certified nursing assistants (CNAs) to work in a nursing home, but certification is not required in all job settings. A nursing assistant may acquire an additional certified medication assistant (CMA) credential, which authorizes him or her to give medications to patients.

Most states do not require that psychiatric technicians hold certification, but certification can enhance a candidate's job prospects. The accrediting organization is called the American Association of Psychiatric Technicians (AAPT). It offers four levels of certification based on education, work experience, and the exam. A level 1 certified psychiatric technician must hold a high school diploma or general equivalency diploma (GED) and pass a certification examination (which is open book and involves 201 multiple-choice questions).

State laws vary widely on certification for substance abuse counselors. A national certification is offered by the National Association for Alcoholism and Drug Abuse Counselors (NAADAC), also known as the Association for Addiction Professionals. In order to be certified as a national certified addiction counselor, level I (NCAC I), a counselor must hold a high school diploma or GED as well as a state credential or license. He or she must also have at least three years of supervised job experience and 270 hours of relevant education or training. The candidate must also pass an exam.

# Chapter 4

# LANDING THE JOB

**H**unting for your first full-time job in mental health care might seem like an overwhelming prospect, but hard work and persistence will yield results. You should begin your job search preparation even before you finish your education or training program. Identify your preferred health care workplace, whether it is a hospital, residential facility, clinic, or other setting, and research potential employers in your area.

To land your first job, you should consider hunting for employment to be a job in itself. Take an organized and methodical approach. You should keep records of possible job openings, positions you've applied for, and contact information of professionals in the field. Get in touch with people who may give you a reference, such as former professors, supervisors, or coworkers. Keep a to-do list for your job search, and don't get discouraged. Spend time every day reviewing, updating, and expanding your search.

## Career Resources

If you start a job search as a student or recent graduate, you might begin with a visit to your school's career

Healthcare Staffing

## Healthcare Professionals

Advance your career and earn what you deserve.

**Immediate Opportunities:**

▷ Nursing     ▷ Respiratory Therapy

▷ Diagnostic Imaging     ▷ Medical Financial

▷ Clinical Laboratory     ▷ Physical Therapy

Health care job fairs offer an opportunity to apply for jobs in the field as well as to network with other health care professionals.

resource center. You'll be able to view job listings and take advantage of various services for job seekers, from résumé tips to workshops on acing an interview. Your teachers and former classmates may be able to share news about job openings in the field as well. Be sure to ask former professors, supervisors, or advisors for letters of recommendation to potential employers, and check whether they would be willing to serve as a reference.

Check out career fairs in your area. Your school may hold a job fair attended by representatives from companies that are hiring across a range of fields. At a health care job fair, you can meet recruiters from area hospitals and other health care employers. Dress professionally for a job fair—you want to make a good first impression—and take along extra copies of your résumé.

Public libraries can also provide valuable career resources. Check the shelves for health care career guides and books on job search strategies. Look at the job listings in newspapers and professional journals, and ask librarians about online career tools available on library computers. Some libraries may offer employment assistance such as workshops or informational sessions with career experts.

A wealth of tools and information for job seekers is available online. Browse the health care sections of huge general career sites as well as health care–specific career sites. You can generally narrow down the location to identify jobs in your region. Professional associations relevant to your specialization may also list job openings in the field. Look at the websites of employers in your area who may be hiring health care personnel. Most big companies—and government agencies—have a job opportunities section. If you hope to land a job with a specific employer, take the initiative to send your résumé to the human resources department even if there aren't any current openings. The human resources manager may keep your résumé on file and contact you when the institution is hiring.

## Using Your Network

If you're new to the job market, you might be intimidated by the prospect of professional networking. But you should realize that you're already surrounded by a support network

If you have an opportunity to attend a health care networking event, conduct yourself professionally and work to make a positive first impression.

of family, friends, colleagues, and casual acquaintances. They would all be happy to let you know of any job openings they are aware of or introduce you to a contact they are acquainted with in your field. Take advantage of the expertise of the people in your network. Ask them what you might expect for an entry-level salary at a given workplace, for example, as well as hours, benefits such as health insurance, and job requirements.

As your career progresses, you will no doubt develop a wider professional network in your mental health care

# INTERVIEWING TO BE A MEDICAL ASSISTANT

An interviewer is likely to ask questions that examine your basic qualifications as well as gauge whether you would be a good match for the workplace. Dona DeZube, a careers expert for Monster.com, provided some common questions that a candidate interviewing to be a medical assistant might expect to hear. (Note: HIPAA—the 1996 Health Insurance Portability and Accountability Act—requires that health care workers protect the confidentiality of certain patient information. OSHA—Occupational Safety and Health Administration—training addresses workplace safety. Phlebotomy is the process of drawing blood.)

- Are you a certified medical assistant?
- What experience do you have with Medent (or other electronic medical records software)?
- What other software are you proficient with?
- Which insurances have you billed?
- Tell me about your HIPAA knowledge.
- What OSHA training have you taken?
- What front-office tasks did you handle in your last position?

- **What phlebotomy skills do you have?**
- **Are you certified in CPR [cardiopulmo-nary resuscitation]?**
- **What phone and voice-mail systems have you used?**
- **Have you taken patient histories, or did your doctor like to do that herself?**
- **What was the scope of your duties in your last practice?**
- **What procedures have you assisted the doctor with?**
- **What decisions were you able to make on your own at your past practice?**
- **How many other techs and medical assistants did you work with in your last job?**
- **Tell me about a time when you had an irate patient.**
- **How do you handle stress?**

**Being prepared to answer questions such as these or others that you might think are relevant to the actual job for which you are interviewing will give you an advantage over other candidates who are competing for the job.**

specialization. Your network will include coworkers and supervisors. As you gain seniority, it will also include junior colleagues, who may ask you for advice and references.

New job seekers might not be aware that many job openings are filled without ever being listed. You might be able to learn of some jobs through your network of contacts from educational programs or work experience such as internships.

Social networking sites can also be a valuable resource. Business-oriented social networking sites offer job services and the opportunity to establish professional relationships with colleagues online. Personal social networks can be useful for maintaining connections with health care colleagues as well.

Be aware of your digital footprint, the impression created by your online activities, however. Employers often check the social media presence and online activities of job candidates. Your social media profile can be a valuable asset if it emphasizes your personal and professional achievements and demonstrates that you have a good work ethic. Use privacy settings so that access to private posts and personal photos is restricted to family and close friends.

## Acing the Interview

If a potential employer is impressed by your application, the next step is the job interview. Companies sometimes screen applicants by setting up an initial phone interview. The face-to-face interview at the workplace, however, is your best opportunity to sell yourself and convince the employer that you're well qualified and ready for the job.

Prepare thoroughly for the interview ahead of time. Review the description of the job requirements and responsibilities and gather some background information

During a job interview, potential employers look for candidates who are confident, capable, and motivated to do their best at the position.

about the workplace. Make a note of any questions you have about working conditions and what to expect as an employee.

Research typical job interview questions and rehearse your answers in a mock interview with a friend. For an open-ended question such as "tell me about yourself," you might reply with a brief description of your professional and educational history, perhaps highlighting an exceptional skill that might give you an advantage over other candidates. Interviewers often ask about short-term and

A candidate for a job should prepare for tough potential interview questions by having answers ready that will highlight his skills and achievements.

long-term career goals or what a candidate considers his or her greatest strengths and weaknesses. Keep your answers professional and emphasize your qualifications and accomplishments.

Get a good night's rest the night before the interview and eat breakfast so that you're not distracted by being hungry. Have your outfit picked out ahead of time. Dress professionally— business suits are appropriate for both men and women, although women may opt for a blouse and perhaps a blazer with slacks or a skirt. Don't show up dressed casually, which might send the message that you don't take the interview seriously. Plan to arrive about fifteen minutes early for the interview.

The job interview is your chance to make a great first impression. Emphasize how your education and work experience are a good fit for the job requirements. Stay positive during the interview—prospective employers are looking for someone who will bring a positive attitude to the workplace. Don't be tempted to exaggerate or lie about your accomplishments or work experience. Acknowledge that you recognize that mental health care can be a challenging field, and emphasize your willingness to learn and improve on the job. Be aware of your body language. Don't slouch or fidget. Smile when you shake hands, and occasionally make eye contact when you're talking.

After the interview, follow up with a thank-you note or email. Reiterate that you think you're a good match for the job and that you're excited at the prospect of joining the team. If you don't hear back from the employer, wait at least a week before making a follow-up call to ask whether the position has been filled.

If you made a good impression during your initial interview, the next step will be a callback. You might undergo multiple rounds of interviews with a prospective employer. Even after the employer decides to make you a job offer, you may go through one last interview.

Meanwhile, keep up the job search. Assess your performance at the job interview and identify any points you could improve on next time. Don't be discouraged if you're not offered the position—a job search is an ongoing process that you might have to refine before you get an offer.

# Chapter 5

# MAPPING YOUR CAREER PATH

anding a new job can be exciting and daunting. Your first job is a milestone in your life and a starting point of your career path. Eventually, your experience and work record will serve as valuable assets in taking on higher-level positions with more responsibilities that offer higher pay.

A first job is a learning experience. Once you've started your job in mental health care, you'll probably begin doing some of the most basic tasks. As you gain expertise and prove your aptitude for hands-on work, your supervisors will entrust you with assignments that require more responsibility. Maintain a positive attitude and an enthusiasm for learning more about the work going on around you. Once you've gained confidence on the job, you might discover that you have aptitudes or interests related to the job that could open up new career opportunities.

## Making a Good Impression

The first days, weeks, and months of your first job are crucial in making a good impression and establishing

Your early days on the job will be a learning period. You'll gain confidence as you grow accustomed to the workplace routines and get to know your coworkers and patients.

a solid work ethic. On your first day, show up early and well rested. You should expect to begin with a period of orientation and training. You'll meet your coworkers, supervisors, and patients and learn the rules and routines of the workplace. Make sure that you're clear on the expectations and responsibilities of your position, and don't be shy about asking questions.

Starting a new job can be overwhelming, and you should accept that you'll probably make a few mistakes

# ASK THE EXPERT: DONNA MAE DEPOLA, SUBSTANCE ABUSE COUNSELOR

Donna Mae DePola became a credentialed alcohol and substance abuse counselor (CASAC) in the late 1980s after overcoming her own drug addiction. In addition to working as a counselor, she is the founder and president of the Resource Training and Counseling Center, a CASAC training school. The following is part of an interview with DePola on the Careers In Psychology website, about being a substance abuse counselor.

*Where are substance abuse counselors usually employed?*
Most counselors work in the outpatient world. But there are so many different facets to this field. Therapeutic communities are a big factor also ... Many counselors also work in outreach and community based organizations ... as a CASAC there are many opportunities.

*Can you tell us a little bit about what you do as a substance abuse counselor?*

(continued on the next page)

*(continued from the previous page)*

**I feel being a CASAC is not only a job but a lifestyle. How you present yourself to the client has a lot to do with your skills as a counselor. Being upbeat, friendly and engaging on a personal level helps me. I am able to help people because I meet them at their level and I don't judge them or get annoyed at them ... We have to be a mentor and advisor to our clients. We have the power of being examples for them.**

early on. Learn from your missteps and demonstrate that you can handle constructive criticism gracefully. Make the most of your orientation and training—take advantage of every opportunity to learn new skills. Establish a good relationship with your team and work to connect with your patients.

Hospitals and other health care settings can be stressful workplaces, and inevitably, there will be disputes and personality clashes on the job. Try to maintain a friendly and professional attitude, and stay out of unhealthy workplace dynamics. Observe how your colleagues manage tense situations, and be aware of appropriate recourses in case you encounter a problem you can't handle on your own.

Practice good self-care to avoid burnout and ensure that you'll always be able to bring your best to the job. Medical settings are notorious for harboring germs, so be sure to wash your hands frequently and take any other necessary steps to avoid spreading infection. Take precautions to avoid injuries, and have injuries reported and treated if you are hurt on the job. Take initiative in dealing with workplace stress as well. Eat a healthy diet, get plenty of exercise, and pursue rewarding activities outside of work. It's important that you maintain a balance between your professional and personal life, too. Mental health care workers must have compassion for their patients, but professional detachment is necessary to avoid becoming overwhelmed by patients' needs and problems.

## Networking and Advancement

Even as you settle into your new job, you should continue thinking about your long-term career goals. As you learn more about the different roles of the members of your team and the other health care professionals around, you may begin to recognize new potential opportunities that you hadn't previously considered. It not uncommon for career plans to change as people gain more real-world knowledge of the workplace. As you refine your career goals, weigh the pros and cons of any prospective changes in your professional life.

Continue expanding your network, and keep in touch with the people who have helped you in the past. In addition to your new circle of colleagues,

Working in the field of health care requires lifelong learning, as new technology and advances in medicine bring about changes in how patients are treated.

you'll probably make contact with others in the field through conferences or other events. Consider joining a professional organization. Professional organizations work to promote the profession and improve the prospects of members. They offer professional development opportunities, career resources, and the opportunity to earn credentials. They may advocate for changes to improve the work life of members of the profession and the quality of health care overall.

Continuing education is essential for health care professionals. New laws are enacted, technology evolves, and health care practices change. Many medical professionals are required to be recertified every couple of years to keep their credentials current. Often, they must complete a specified number of hours of education or training as part of the process. Try keeping up-to-date in the field by reading journals, newsletters, and online articles related to mental health.

You might consider improving your prospects in your field by attaining higher levels of certification. To become certified as a level 2 psychiatric technician, for example, a candidate must complete 480 hours of college or university courses and work in the field for a year. A level 3 psychiatric technician must complete 480 hours of course work and work in the field for two years. A level 4 psychiatric technician must hold a bachelor's degree in mental health or developmental disabilities and work in the field for three years. All higher levels of certification also require passing the basic exam and completing an essay exam on situations a psychiatric technician might encounter on the job. A substance abuse counselor may consider higher levels of certification or gaining certification for treating specific addictions.

Another possible career pathway could involve obtaining additional education and training to qualify in a related field of health care. A nursing assistant, for example, might train to become a licensed practical nurse. A licensed practical nurse might train to become

Experienced health care workers may be promoted to roles with greater responsibilities. A higher-level psychiatric technician, for example, may be granted more authority in determining patient treatment plans.

a registered nurse. A registered nurse may train to receive certification as a psychiatric nurse or substance abuse nurse. Hospitals will often help pay for employees' continuing education and training.

Yet another attractive career path is advancement to management roles. Experienced personnel who have demonstrated that they can handle responsibility and provide effective leadership may be promoted to supervisory or administrative positions. Pursuing additional education and training is likely to improve your prospects for advancement.

No matter what specialization or career path you pursue, mental health care is a field that offers considerable opportunities for dedicated professionals who want to help people. Professionals working in mental health care acknowledge that the work is challenging and requires a sincere commitment. But they also say that the rewards of the work—seeing patients change their lives for the better because of their efforts and those of other mental health care workers—make the work uniquely fulfilling.

# GLOSSARY

**bachelor's degree** The undergraduate degree obtained after completing a four-year college program.

**certification** The awarding of a certificate or license upon completion of a course of study or passing of an exam.

**counselor** Someone trained to provide guidance on personal, social, or psychological problems.

**credential** Proof, usually written, that demonstrates someone's identity, authority, or qualifications.

**diagnose** To identify the nature of a medical condition by examining the symptoms.

**examination** In medicine, a physical inspection of the patient's body performed in order to assess health.

**hygiene** Practices such as cleanliness that promote good health and prevent disease.

**internship** A short-term training job, generally completed to gain practical experience.

**license** Official permission from the government or other authority, such as those that allow one to practice a trade.

**management** The executives or administrators who direct and operate a business or organization.

**master's degree** An advanced degree obtained after completing a one- or two-year graduate program.

**network** To maintain communication with a group of people, especially to exchange information about professional opportunities.

**reference** Someone who provides a statement of professional qualifications; also, the statement itself.

**rehabilitation** The act of restoring or bringing someone to a healthy condition.

**relapse** To return or slip back to a previous state or behavior.

**résumé** A summary of one's professional qualifications and work experience.

**stress** Strain or tension, involving mental, emotional, and physical responses.

**technician** Someone trained in practical applications and knowledge, especially of a mechanical or scientific subject.

**therapy** Treatment of mental health problems.

**vital signs** Clinical measurements, such as body temperature and blood pressure, that indicate a patient's general physical condition.

**volunteer** To participate in unpaid work.

# FOR MORE INFORMATION

American Association of Psychiatric Technicians
    (AAPT)
1220 S Street, Suite 100
Sacramento, CA 95811
(800) 391-7589
Website: https://psychtechs.org
The AAPT awards national certification to psychiatric
    technicians. The organization also provides informa-
    tion about the profession and test preparation
    resources.

American Nurses Association (ANA)
8515 Georgia Avenue, Suite 400
Silver Spring, MD 20910
(800) 274-4262
Website: http://www.nursingworld.org
Facebook: @AmericanNursesAssociation
Twitter: @ANANursingWorld
The ANA promotes the interests of those in the nursing
    field by advocating for the rights and welfare of
    nurses, providing professional development
    resources, establishing standards for the profession,
    and awarding credentials.

American Psychological Association (APA)
750 First Street NE
Washington, DC 20002-4242
(800) 374-2721
Website: http://www.apa.org
Facebook: @AmericanPsychologicalAssociation
Twitter: @apa

The APA is a scientific and professional organization representing psychologists. It also educates the public about psychology, behavioral science, and mental health.

Bureau of Labor Statistics (BLS)
US Department of Labor
2 Massachusetts Avenue NE, Suite 2135
Washington, DC 20212-0001
(202) 691-5700
Website: http://www.bls.gov
This federal agency analyzes labor market activity, industry working conditions, and price changes in the US economy. Every year, the BLS updates the *Occupational Outlook Handbook* (https://www.bls.gov/ooh), which describes thousands of careers, including those relating to the mental health field, with details about job requirements and average salaries.

Canadian Mental Health Association (CMHA)
1110-151 Slater Street
Ottawa, ON K1P 5H3
Canada
Website: http://www.cmha.ca
Facebook and Instagram: @CMHANational
Twitter: @CMHA_NTL
The CMHA is the organization dedicated to supporting the mental health of Canadians and providing services to people experiencing mental illness.

Health Canada
Address Locator 0900C2
Ottawa, ON K1A 0K9
Canada
(613) 957-2991
Website: https://www.canada.ca/en/health
-canada.html
Facebook: @HealthyCdns and
@HealthyFirstNationsandInuit
Twitter: @GovCanHealth
Health Canada is the Canadian government's depart-
ment that is responsible for safeguarding the public's
health. It includes services and information related
to mental health concerns, such as maintaining
good mental health and recognizing mental illness.

Health eCareers
6465 South Greenwood Plaza Boulevard, Suite 400
Centennial, CO 80111
(888) 884-8242
Website: https://www.healthecareers.com
Facebook: @HealtheCareers
Twitter: @Healthecareers
Health eCareers is a health care industry career site for
professionals, providers, and associations, aiming
to match qualified health care job seekers with
career opportunities.

Mental Health America (MHA)
500 Montgomery Street, Suite 820

Alexandria, VA 22314
(703) 684-7722
Website: http://www.mentalhealthamerica.net
Facebook, Instagram, and Twitter: @
  mentalhealthamerica
The MHA is a community-based nonprofit organization
  that helps offer treatment and support to individuals
  with mental illness and advocates for policies that
  promote mental health and well-being.

NAADAC, the Association for Addiction Professionals
44 Canal Center Plaza, Suite 301
Alexandria, VA  22314
(703) 741-7686
Website: https://www.naadac.org
Facebook: @Naadac
Twitter: @NAADACorg
The NAADAC is the professional organization that
  provides educational resources, awards credentials,
  and advocates for the interests of addiction counselors in the United States, Canada, and internationally.

# FOR FURTHER READING

Culp, Jennifer. *Jump-Starting Careers as Medical Assistants and Certified Nursing Assistants* (Health Care Careers in 2 Years). New York, NY: Rosen Publishing, 2014.

Freedman, Jeri. *Jump-Starting a Career in Hospitals & Home Health Care* (Health Care Careers in 2 Years). New York, NY: Rosen Publishing, 2014.

Fry, Ron. *Surefire Tips to Improve Your Organization Skills* (Surefire Study Success). New York, NY: Rosen Publishing, 2016.

Fry, Ron. *Surefire Tips to Improve Your Study Skills* (Surefire Study Success). New York, NY: Rosen Publishing, 2016.

Harmon, Daniel E. *Careers in Mental Health* (Essential Careers). New York, NY: Rosen Publishing, 2013.

Hodges, Shannon. *101 Careers in Counseling.* 2nd ed. New York, NY: Springer Publishing, 2018.

Hubbard, Rita L. *What Degree Do I Need to Pursue a Career in Health Care?* (The Right Degree for Me). New York, NY: Rosen Publishing, 2015.

Metz, Kim. *Careers in Mental Health: Opportunities in Psychology, Counseling, and Social Work.* Malden, MA: John Wiley and Sons, 2016.

Morkes, Andrew. *Hot Health Care Careers: 30 Occupations with Fast Growth and Many New Job Openings.* 2nd ed. Chicago, IL: College & Career Press, 2017.

Reeves, Diane Lindsey. *Health Sciences: Exploring Career Pathways.* Ann Arbor, MI: Cherry Lake Publishing, 2017.

Ritter, Jessica A., and Halaevalu F. O. Vakalahi. *101 Careers in Social Work.* 2nd ed. New York, NY: Springer Publishing, 2014.

Roland, James. *Careers in Mental Health* (Exploring Careers). San Diego, CA: ReferencePoint Press, 2017.

Sheen, Barbara. *Careers in Health Care* (Exploring Careers). San Diego, CA: ReferencePoint Press, 2015.

Sternberg, Robert J., ed. *Career Paths in Psychology: Where Your Degree Can Take You*. 3rd ed. Washington, DC: American Psychological Association, 2017.

# BIBLIOGRAPHY

American Association of Psychiatric Technicians. "The Certification Process." Retrieved February 2, 2018. https://psychtechs.org/the-certification-process.

Bureau of Labor Statistics. "Psychiatric Technicians and Aides." *Occupational Outlook Handbook*, January 30, 2018. https://www.bls.gov/ooh/healthcare /psychiatric-technicians-and-aides.htm#tab-1.

Bureau of Labor Statistics. "Substance Abuse, Behavioral Disorders, and Mental Health Counselors." *Occupational Outlook Handbook*, January 30, 2018. https://www.bls.gov/ooh/community-and-social -service/substance-abuse-behavioral-disorder-and -mental-health-counselors.htm.

Careers in Psychology. "Donna Mae DePola: Substance Abuse Counselor." Retrieved February 9, 2018. https://careersinpsychology.org/interview/donna -mae-depola.

DeZube, Dona. "Prepare for a Medical Assistant Interview." Monster.com. Retrieved February 9, 2018. https://www.monster.com/career-advice/article /medical-assistant-interview-preparation.

Enelow, Wendy S., and Louise M. Kursmark. *Expert Resumes for Health Careers*. 2nd ed. Indianapolis, IN: Jist Works, 2010.

Ferguson. *Exploring Health Care Careers*. 3rd ed. New York, NY: Ferguson, 2006.

Ferguson. *What Can I Do Now? Health Care*. New York, NY: Ferguson, 2007.

Field, Shelly. *Career Opportunities in Health Care*. 3rd ed. New York, NY: Checkmark Books, 2007.

Gifford, Steven. "Differences Between Outpatient and Inpatient Treatment Programs." Psych Central, July 17,

2016. https://psychcentral.com/lib/differences
-between-outpatient-and-inpatient-treatment-programs.
Graduate School of Addiction Studies. "How to Become
an Addiction Counselor." Hazelden Betty Ford
Foundation, October 5, 2017. http://www
.hazeldenbettyford.org/articles/graduate-school
/how-to-become-a-substance-abuse-counselor.
Health Care Jobs Start Here. "A Day in the Life."
Retrieved February 6, 2018. http://www
.healthjobsstarthere.com/dayinthelife/toni.
Longton, Jacqueline, "A Look at Violence in the
Workplace Against Psychiatric Aides and Psychiatric
Technicians." *Monthly Labor Review*, US Bureau of
Labor Statistics, March 2015. https://www.bls.gov
/opub/mlr/2015/article/a-look-at-violence-in-the
-workplace-against-psychiatric-aides-and-psychiatric
-technicians.htm.
Mental Health America. "Mental Health Treatments."
Retrieved February 2, 2018. http://www
.mentalhealthamerica.net/types-mental-health
-treatments.
National Alliance on Mental Health. "Mental Health by
the Numbers." Retrieved February 2, 2018. https://
www.nami.org/Learn-More/Mental-Health
-By-the-Numbers.
Public Relation Staff. "A Day in the Life of a Mental Health
Technician." Akron Children's Hospital, July 31, 2014.
http://inside.akronchildrens.org/2014/07/31
/a-day-in-the-life-of-a-mental-health-technician.
Quan, Kathy. *The Everything Guide to Careers in Health
Care: Find the Job That's Right for You.* Avon, MA:
Adams Media, 2007.

Substance Abuse and Mental Health Services
Administration. "Treatments for Substance Use
Disorders." August 9, 2016. https://www.samhsa
.gov/treatment/substance-use-disorders.
Waters, Brad. "23 Mental Health Professionals
Interviewed About Their Jobs." *Psychology Today*,
June 24, 2015. https://www.psychologytoday.com
/blog/design-your-path/201506/23-mental-health
-professionals-interviewed-about-their-jobs.
Wischnitzer, Saul, and Edith Wischnitzer. *Top 100 Health-
Care Careers: Your Complete Guidebook to Training
and Jobs in Allied Health, Nursing, Medicine, and
More.* 3rd ed. Indianapolis, IN: Jist Works, 2011.

# INDEX

## About the Author

Corona Brezina has written numerous nonfiction books for young adults. Among her books that have focused on teen mental health issues and in-demand careers are *Everything You Need to Know About Anger Management; Getting a Job in Health Care; Careers in Digital Media; and Top STEM Careers in Math.* She lives in Chicago.

## Photo Credits

Cover (figure) Alexander Raths/Shutterstock.com; cover (background) Suwin/Shutterstock.com; back cover, p. 1 (background graphic) HunThomas/Shutterstock.com; pp. 4–5 (background) and interior pages Africa Studio/Shutterstock.com; p. 5 (inset) ERproductions Ltd/Blend Images/Getty Images; p. 9 Tom M Johnson/Blend Images/Getty Images; pp. 12, 49 Hero Images/Getty Images; p. 16 Peter Dazeley/Photographer's Choice/Getty Images; p. 19 © Mary Kate Denny/PhotoEdit; p. 22 DenGuy/E+/Getty Images; p. 24 Alpa Prod/Shutterstock.com; p. 27 Vstock/UpperCut Images/Getty Images; p. 29 MBI/Alamy Stock Photo; p. 31 alvarez/E+/Getty Images; p. 34 ImageFlow/Shutterstock.com; pp. 37, 54–55, 64 Steve Debenport/E+/Getty Images; pp. 39, 53 sturti/E+/Getty Images; p. 43 fstop123/E+/Getty Images; p. 47 Justin Sullivan/Getty Images; p. 58 Jochen Sands/DigitalVision/Thinkstock; p. 62 Matej Kastelic/Shutterstock.com.

Design: Michael Moy; Layout: Ellina Litmanovich; Senior Editor: Kathy Kuhtz Campbell; Photo Researcher: Karen Huang